CHAMPIONS AT BAT

THREE POWER HITTERS

BY ANN FINLAYSON

ILLUSTRATED BY PAUL FRAME

GARRARD PUBLISHING COMPANY
CHAMPAIGN, ILLINOIS

*To the Amazin's:
the New York Mets, 1969*

Sports Consultant:
COLONEL RED REEDER
Former Member of the West Point Coaching Staff
and
Former Special Assistant to the West Point
Director of Athletics

Photo credits:
Brown Brothers: p. 23, 38, 58, 64 (top), 70, 88, 94
Culver Pictures, Inc.: p. 19
United Press International: p. 4, 30, 31, 48, 52
Wide World Photos: p. 36 (both), 64 (bottom), 81 (both), 84, 86 (both)

Copyright © 1970 by Ann Finlayson
All rights reserved. Manufactured in the U.S.A.
Standard Book Number: 8116-6661-1
Library of Congress Catalog Card Number: 74-113838

Contents

The Hard-Driving Rajah:
　　Rogers Hornsby 5

Into Babe Ruth's Shoes:
　　Joe DiMaggio 39

All He's Got:
　　Ted Williams 71

The Hard-Driving Rajah: Rogers Hornsby

Manager Miller Huggins of the St. Louis Cardinals saw his new shortstop approaching. Rogers Hornsby was a good-looking Texas boy, tall and lanky. He always said what he thought—no punches pulled, everything out in the open.

"Hug," he asked frankly, "what are my chances for next year?"

Manager Huggins wasn't sure what answer to give the earnest nineteen year old. For the last three weeks of the 1915 season, Rogers had been trying out for a place on the St. Louis team. He had not been playing up to major-league standards.

"Well, Rogers," the manager said finally, "you've got plenty of fire and ambition, and I like that. But there's not enough weight behind your batting swing. These major-league pitchers have you handcuffed."

"Does that mean I'm fired?"

"Not exactly. To tell you the truth, Rogers, I think you need to be farmed out until you get more weight and seasoning."

"Farmed out?" repeated Hornsby.

"That's right. I'm telling you for your own good."

When Huggins said "farmed out," he meant "returned to the minor leagues." He felt that young Hornsby needed a year or two of experience before he entered major-league competition. But the Texas boy thought the manager was talking about a real farm.

"I'll see what I can do," he promised.

He walked away, his mind turning over rapidly. There was his uncle's farm in Caldwell County, Texas. He'd go there and work hard, and maybe next spring he'd make good.

He *had* to make good. The only thing Rogers Hornsby had ever wanted to do with his life was to be a big-league ballplayer. And the only way he knew how to get there was to work.

His mother had taught him that, back in West Texas where he was born in 1896. There had been five children in the Hornsby family and not much money. Everybody had had to work hard.

But the Hornsbys all played hard, too, and their favorite game was baseball. Rogers would walk five miles or more to get into a game. Sometimes he played in two

or three games in one day. "Baseball, baseball," his mother often sighed. "That boy thinks of nothing else."

Rogers was ten when he got his first job. He worked as a messenger boy for a local packinghouse. To his delight the company had a baseball team, and he wheedled the players into making him bat boy. Sometimes they even let him play.

"You know, that kid is *good*," the team captain said one day. After that, when a player had to miss a game, they let Rogers fill in. By the time he was twelve he had played almost every position on the team.

The Hornsbys were living in Fort Worth by then. "Mom, I need a baseball uniform," Rogers told his mother one day. "I just joined the North Side Athletics."

"Another team?" cried Mrs. Hornsby.

"Yes, I need the practice." The boy looked at her with a serious expression. "Mom," he said slowly, "do you think I could be a big-leaguer some day?"

"Why, I don't know, Rogers," she answered. "But if you have talent, work is what will bring it out."

Rogers nodded, taking the words to heart.

Mrs. Hornsby could see how much the game meant to him. She found some old blue flannel and made it into uniforms for the team. When Rogers needed sliding pads, she cut up an old quilt. She encouraged him.

Rogers drove himself hard. When he was eighteen, he was given a tryout with a Class D team in a small town. That team soon folded, but Rogers was sold to the club at Denison, Texas. He was still raw and clumsy and overeager. He made an error in every two or three games. But he worked hard to correct his faults.

He was playing shortstop at Denison when a Cardinals scout first saw him. The scout was impressed with his dash and drive. So, in September, 1915, Rogers reported to St. Louis for his big chance. He had tried hard, but he wasn't surprised when Miller Huggins said he needed farming out.

Rogers spent the winter of 1916 on his uncle's farm. He did chores, tended livestock, and mended fences. He slept twelve hours every night. He ate eggs and fried chicken and biscuits. And in his spare time he worked at his batting swing.

At spring training time, Rogers reported to the Cardinals' camp, twenty-five pounds heavier. Miller Huggins hardly recognized him. When Rogers explained what he had done, the manager laughed. "Maybe your idea of 'farmed out' is better than mine," he admitted. "Here's a bat. Get up there and show me what you can do."

Rogers stepped up to the plate. He had been advised to choke up on the bat. "Only really powerful hitters can swing from the tip," Manager Huggins had often told him. Now, however, Rogers decided to do it his own way.

He slid his hands down to the end of the bat. He stood as far from the plate as possible, his heels touching the rim of the batter's box. He took a practice swing.

"All right, blaze one in there," he called to the pitcher.

The pitcher grinned at Huggins and pitched a hot one right down the middle.

Rogers stepped into it, his husky arms bringing the bat around hard and fast. There was a mighty *crack!*

Huggins' jaw dropped. So did the pitcher's. The little white ball was still rising as it cleared the outfield fence.

Rogers tried it again and again, while Huggins watched. The extra weight had indeed given young Hornsby added power. Finally Huggins called, "All right, kid, that's enough for today." He said nothing more about sending Rogers back to the minor leagues.

By the end of the 1916 season, Rogers Hornsby had a batting average of .313 and was in the big leagues to stay.

Once Rogers was sure that he was a full-fledged Cardinal, he made up his mind to become the best batter around. Day after day he worked at his batting. He listened to Manager Huggins' advice, but in the end Rogers developed a style that was like nobody else's.

"Look at Hornsby," said a St. Louis fan,

watching him play. "How can he hit, standing so far back in the box? Most batters crowd the plate."

"When the pitch comes," he explained, "I know just where to expect it. Then I can step in and get my full power behind the swing." Unlike many power hitters, Rogers could hit to all fields.

He batted right-handed, which was supposed to be a slight handicap. First base is one step farther away from a right-hander than from a left. But Rogers refused to switch.

"Most great batters hit left," he was warned.

He shrugged it off. "This is the right way for me."

Rogers put everything he had into baseball. He would not play golf, because he was afraid it would hurt his swing. He avoided movies to protect his eyesight. He

did not drink or smoke, because he wanted to keep in top condition.

He worked to improve his fielding. He tried playing second base and third base and even the outfield. Finally he settled down for good at second base. Soon the awkward boy who had been troubled by errors was being called baseball's finest second baseman.

"Look how he makes that across-the-chest throw!" one sportswriter said to another. "That's one of the toughest throws in baseball."

"Hornsby sure rips it off smooth as silk."

In 1918, Miller Huggins went to the New York Yankees. He was replaced the following season by another great manager, Branch Rickey. Rickey liked to lecture to his team, diagraming plays on a blackboard. Rogers had great respect for both Huggins and Rickey, but he had his own ideas about how the game should be played.

"You have to drive every minute," he told a teammate. "You have to fight for every run."

Rogers studied every angle of the game, every technique. He made himself familiar with the weak points and strong points of every player. But he never neglected his batting. Hard years of practice slowly built up his average. In 1920, when he had boosted it to .370, Rogers won his first batting championship.

Up till then, few people outside St. Louis had been interested in Rogers Hornsby. But nobody can ignore a champion. "There he is," fans pointed out to one another. "Look at him swing that bat!"

"Come on, Hornsby!" the Cards' rooters cheered. "Rogers the Rajah! You're king of batters in this league!"

The name spread, and soon fans were saying, "Here comes the Rajah! The Rajah will knock in this run. Come on, Rajah!"

Rogers lived up to his new nickname. In 1921, he pushed his average up to .397. The following year he hit .401. That magic .400 mark had been topped only twelve times in major-league history. But Rogers was not content to do it once. Twice more he racked up averages in the .400's. In 1921, the Texas slugger finished the season with an average of .424. Nearly half a century later, that figure still stands as the modern record.

On May 31, 1925, Hornsby was called into the Cardinals' head office. "Rogers," said the club owner, "Rickey is moving up to the business end of the game. How would you like to be manager in his place?"

The husky Texan stared at his boss. "But I'm just a hitter, a slugger."

Rogers Hornsby, left, who hit .401 in 1922, talks with another great hitter, Babe Ruth.

"We think you're a lot more than that. How about it?"

Rogers didn't need to think it over for long. "I want the job," he said.

Grimly the new manager considered his problems. The Cardinals had never won a pennant. In early 1925 they were in last place. Branch Rickey had good ideas, but his leadership was weak. All along, Rogers had thought the Cardinals needed push. Now he was going to see that they got it.

Hornsby became a driving leader, demanding the best from his players. One day an outfielder dawdled and missed a catch. At the end of the inning, the manager cornered the man. "You're playing rotten ball," Rogers told him bluntly. "If I don't see some improvement, you're off the club."

He saw some improvement.

But only Rogers could say things like that. He let no outsiders interfere with his authority. When a club owner tried to give him some baseball advice, Rogers said, "Listen, you take care of the stock market, and I'll take care of the team."

Many people resented this outspokenness. Others believed that Rogers' methods were good for the team.

The Cardinals finished the 1925 season in fourth place. Their new manager hit .403 and won his sixth batting championship in a row. St. Louis fans began to get their hopes up. "Wait till next year," they promised one another. "If the Rajah keeps on this way, we'll have that pennant yet."

Rogers' hopes were high, too, but he knew it wouldn't be easy. The Pittsburgh Pirates, Cincinnati Reds, and New York Giants had all finished ahead of St. Louis the previous year. All three were still strong contenders in 1926. And the Cardinals had an additional handicap: the team management insisted on their playing exhibition games between regular season games.

"My men are worn out," Rogers protested with his usual directness. "They need to rest on off days."

"We need the money," the club owner answered.

"The best way to make money is to have a pennant-winning team. How can we win with worn-out players?"

"I'm sorry, Rogers. The extra games have to be played."

Another man might have used the exhibition games as an excuse for failure. But Rogers responded to every setback with more drive and greater determination. "We'll show them," he told his men angrily. "We'll win that pennant in spite of them."

He made some changes in the lineup and saw that everyone trained hard. In June he talked the front office into buying Grover

Alexander was recruited by the Cards at the age of 39 to add a little muscle to the St. Louis team.

Cleveland Alexander from the Cubs. "Old Pete" Alexander was one of the greatest pitchers of all time. In three separate seasons he had won more than thirty games, a tremendous feat. In six others he had won more than twenty. He tied the immortal Christy Mathewson in total number of games won. In 1926 Alexander was thirty-nine and nearing the end of his pitching career. But Hornsby thought he could help the Cardinals.

The Cardinals started out slowly, but Rogers drove them to be better. He was the heart of the team. He beat out hits, scrambled after double plays, and stretched singles into doubles with daring base running. Most of all, his big bat always seemed to be ready when a hit was needed most.

"Every play counts," he told his players. "I don't want any man on my team who won't give everything he's got."

By midsummer the Giants were out of the running. Throughout August, the race was between the Pirates and the Reds, with the Cardinals slowly catching up. On August 31, St. Louis took first place and held it for four days. On September 4, they lost it to the Reds. The next day, they took it back.

Gradually the Pirates faded out. The last three weeks of the season turned into a neck-and-neck race between the Cardinals and the Cincinnati Reds.

"This is undoubtedly one of the most sensational races the major circuits have ever known," marveled a veteran sports reporter.

On September 13, the St. Louis Cardinals announced that the club was accepting orders for World Series tickets. Perhaps it was too soon. That same day, the team lost a fourteen-inning heartbreaker, and the pennant race was tied.

The next day the Cardinals had to play an exhibition game in New Haven, Connecticut. Between innings, Rogers rushed to the radio for news of the Cincinnati-Brooklyn game. "Come on, Bums!" he rooted. But the Reds won and took the lead.

Two days later, a determined Hornsby led his team onto the field in Philadelphia for a doubleheader. "The Reds are only playing one game today," he told them. "If we win

25

both ends of this one, we'll be even again."

The Cardinals poured onto the field, Hornsby's reminder ringing in their ears. Restlessly, they waited for their chance, and in the third inning it came. One man hit safely, then another, then a third. Before the inning was over, the Cardinals had piled up twelve runs off five pitchers. The game ended 23–3. The second game was another massacre, 10–2.

The Reds had also won, so the race was tied.

On September 17, St. Louis beat the Phillies once more, while the Reds were losing. The Cardinals were back on top, and there they stayed.

On September 24, Hornsby and his men clinched the pennant.

St. Louis went wild with joy. It was raining hard that day, but no one cared. Cars

jammed the streets. Fans threw confetti and straw hats out of windows. Paper streamers hung from telephone wires. Factory whistles blew. Police and fire sirens blared. Strangers danced together in the street.

The weary ballplayers grinned at one another.

But to hard-driving Rogers the job was only half done. "We still have the World Series to win," he pointed out bluntly.

The American League champions that year were the mighty New York Yankees. Their lineup rang with ominous names: Babe Ruth, Tony Lazzeri, Bob Meusel, Lou Gehrig. Their manager was Rogers' old boss, Miller Huggins. All the experts predicted a Yankee victory.

"This powerful New York team will steamroller the Cardinals and their young manager," one reporter wrote confidently.

But Hornsby thought the Cardinals could

win. "We've fought hard all summer against heavy odds," he told newsmen. "You can bet your life we're not going to stop fighting now."

Rogers also had a personal misfortune to battle. Just before the Series started, his mother fell dangerously ill in Texas. Years before, she had helped him get started by making his first uniform. Now she refused to let her last illness draw Rogers home. "Tell him to stay with his team and win," she said firmly just before she died.

The funeral was postponed, and Rogers stayed with the Cardinals.

The Series opened on October 2, in Yankee Stadium. The Yankees won the first game. St. Louis took the second and third games, and the Yankees won the fourth and fifth. When the Cardinals evened the score by winning the sixth game, fans were wild with excitement.

Babe Ruth socks a homer for New York in the exciting 1926 World Series with St. Louis.

The seventh and final game was played in New York. "Here comes Ruth!" cried fans as the great hitter appeared at the plate. The Babe swung, there was a *crack!* and forty thousand New Yorkers screamed with delight.

"A home run! We're ahead!"

But the Cardinals caught up. In the fourth inning, they scored three runs. Two innings later, the Yankees got one more, making the score 3-2. Then came the seventh inning, one of the most memorable in the history of baseball.

Jesse Haines, the Cardinals' pitcher, had a blister on his finger. "Think you can finish the game?" Hornsby asked him anxiously.

"I think so. Let me try."

It was a bad situation, but Hornsby didn't

Tony Lazzeri slides into home plate for another Yankee run in the 1926 Series.

know what else to do. All his pitchers were tired. His best man, "Old Pete" Alexander, had already won two Series games. "All right, Jesse. We'll see how it goes."

Haines managed to get two men out. But then his control went. He walked Ruth, Gehrig, and Combs, the center fielder, filling the bases. The next man up was rugged Tony Lazzeri.

Rogers walked over to the mound. "I'm sorry, Jesse, but I have to pull you out."

He signaled to the bullpen. He had made a risky decision. Alexander had pitched only the day before. But if any man could save the Cardinals, he was it. So Rogers believed.

"Old Pete" ambled out to the mound to meet his boss. "Well, you can see the situation," Rogers said. "The bases are full, and Lazzeri is the hitter. Lazzeri has a runs-batted-in-record that's nearly as good as Babe Ruth's."

"Old Pete" nodded. "I'll handle Lazzeri."

The first pitch was a strike. The second one looked good to Lazzeri, and he swung. The ball went streaking toward the left-field wall, and Yankee fans rose with a shriek. But it landed foul.

"Old Pete" set himself. This was the big

one. He took the sign and went into his windup. The pitch was a low curve. Lazzeri braced himself and stood up to it. *Whiff!*

The umpire jerked up his thumb.

"Old Pete" Alexander had struck him out. And Rogers' faith in the aging pitcher had paid off.

As player, above, Hornsby hits a long drive.
As manager, below, he surveys a high pop.

For two more innings, Alexander kept the mighty Yankees from scoring. When the game ended, the St. Louis Cardinals were world champions.

Rogers Hornsby, with his big bat and his hard driving, had made baseball history.

Hornsby continued to make baseball history. Over the years the Rajah managed four different major-league baseball teams. As late as 1952, he was brought out of retirement to build up the St. Louis Browns.

But it was as a hitter that Rogers Hornsby won his greatest personal fame. His lifetime average of .358 was topped only by that of left-hander Ty Cobb. And only the immortal Cobb shared Hornsby's feat of three times topping .400.

"Rogers Hornsby," say sportswriters, "was the greatest right-handed batsman in the history of the game."

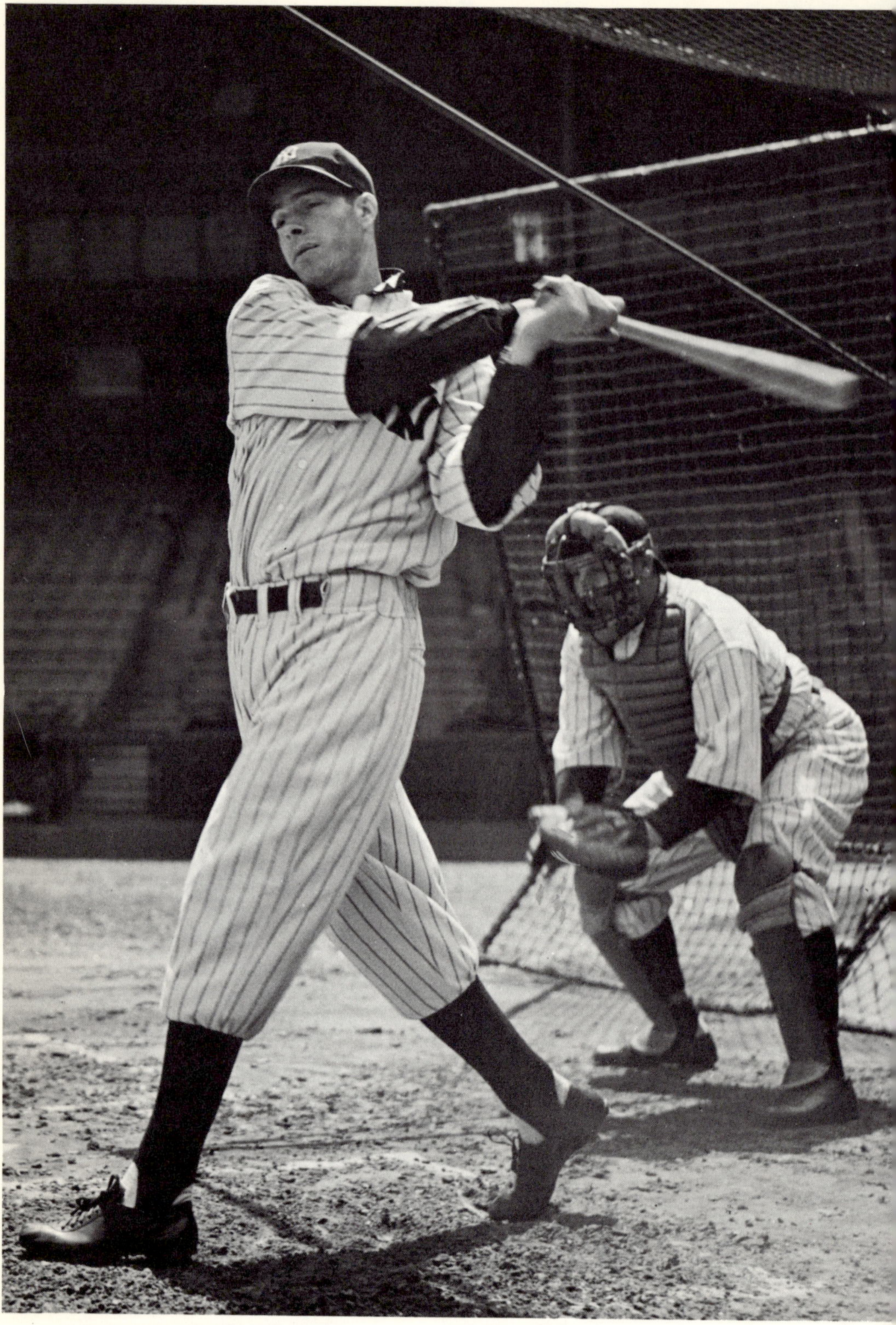

Into Babe Ruth's Shoes: Joe DiMaggio

It was late at night when the phone rang, waking the young ballplayer from slumber. "Who is it?" he inquired sleepily.

The caller was the young man's boss. "I just thought you'd like to hear the news, Joe. You have been bought by the New York Yankees."

Joseph Paul DiMaggio came wide awake. "The Yankees have bought *me?*"

"That's right. Babe Ruth is too old to play another season. They need a new young hitter to step into his shoes. And you're it."

For a moment Joe was too stunned to reply. Then he managed to say, "Well, thanks for telling me. Thanks a lot."

He hung up the receiver and sat back. There would be no more sleep for him that night. He was a Yankee now! What's more, they expected him to be a second Babe Ruth!

As far back as Joe could remember, Babe Ruth had been baseball's biggest star. San Francisco, where Joe lived, was clear across the country from New York. But San Francisco kids knew all about the Babe.

"Hit it like Babe Ruth!" they yelled at one another in those days. "Make it a home run!"

Joe played third base on the neighborhood team. The other four DiMaggio brothers like to play ball, too. So did just about every boy in the North Beach section of San Francisco.

The neighborhood ball field was a vacant lot. The outfield was all rutted with cart tracks. Rocks marked the bases. Fielders made their own gloves out of padded sugar bags. Sometimes the boys had to chip in to buy a ball. But they played a fast, exciting game.

Papa DiMaggio couldn't understand all this excitement about baseball. He was a crab fisherman by trade, working hard to support his nine children. For sport he bowled Italian style.

"I don't like this baseball," he said, shaking his head. "When I need a son to clean my boat, where is he? He's down the street, playing baseball. How can I make fishermen out of lazy baseball players?"

But Joe's mother waved a finger at her husband. "You have your bowling," she scolded. "Let the boys have their baseball."

The two oldest DiMaggio boys, Tom and Mike, became good fishermen like their father. But Vincent, the middle son, got a job in a fruit market and continued playing ball on weekends.

One day Joe's kid brother Dominic came rushing up to him. "Did you hear about Vince?" he cried.

"No, what about him?" Joe wanted to know.

Little Dom was so excited he could hardly stand still. "The Seals have signed him!"

That *was* big news. The San Francisco Seals were one of the best teams in the minor leagues. Many Seal players went right on to the major leagues, which were all in the East and Middle West then.

At supper that night, the two youngsters could hardly take their eyes off their big brother. "Gosh, Vince," Joe said, "maybe you'll be famous some day, like Babe Ruth."

"And what about you, kid?" said the older boy. "It's time *you* started taking baseball seriously."

"Me?"

"You could be good, Joe, if you put your mind to it."

Until then Joe had thought of baseball as a mere game. But Vince's praise set him to wondering. A man could make a career

43

out of baseball if he was good enough. Joe was a modest boy, shy and retiring, but he knew he played good ball.

He joined a Boys' Club team, sponsored by a local businessman. Their sponsor entered them in an industrial league, and they won the championship. Joe played hard.

He was growing into a big, husky youngster with well-muscled arms. His fielding was a little wild, but he wielded a powerful bat. When he was seventeen, the Seals' scout Spike Hennessy saw him.

"You've got a lot of promise, kid," he said. "You want to work out with the team, so we can look you over?"

"You mean it, Mr. Hennessy?"

"Sure thing, Joe. It's not like being on the team, but you can learn a thing or two watching your big brother."

For a few weeks, the two DiMaggios practiced together. Then came the last three

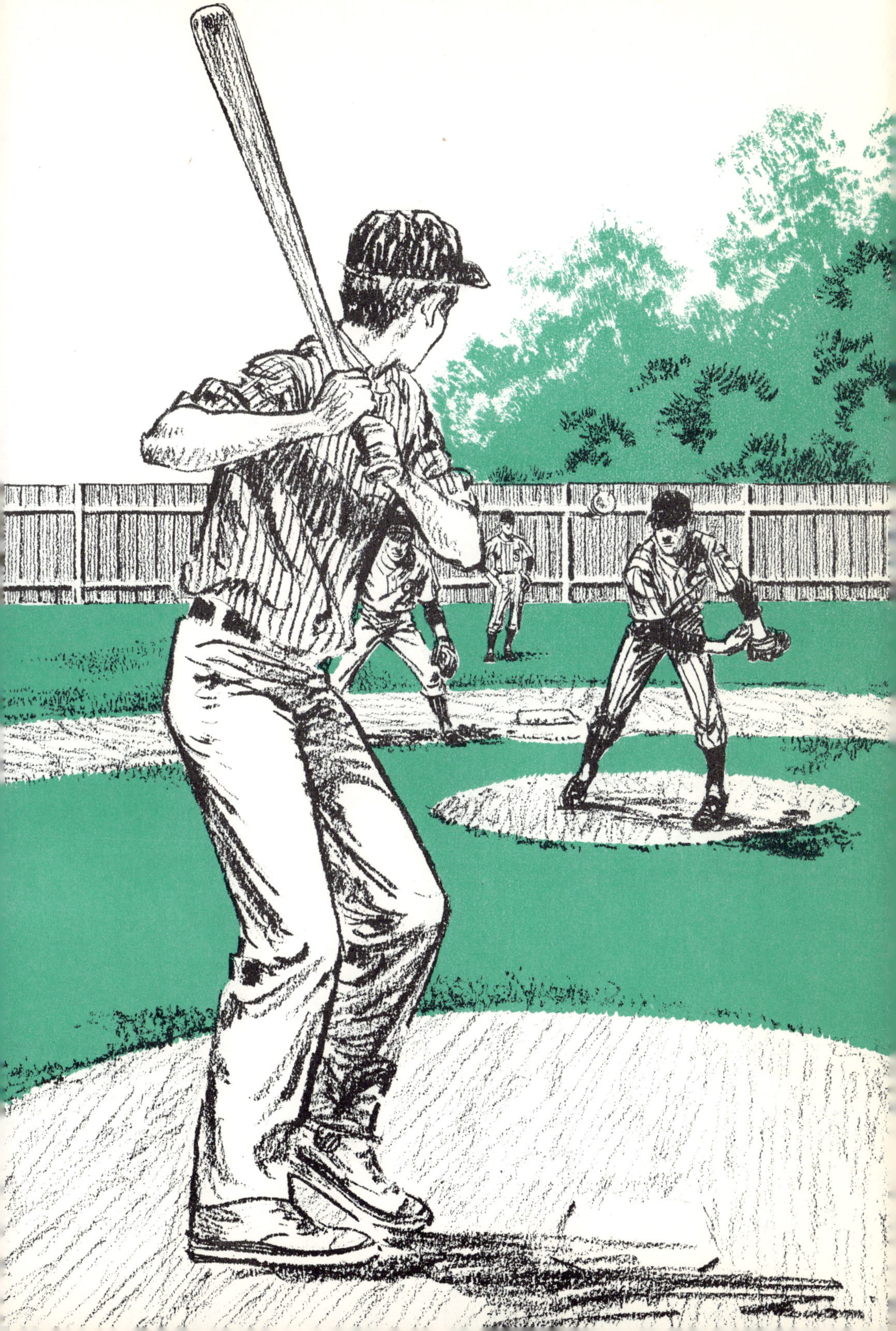

games of the season. The regular shortstop wanted to take off early. Manager Ike Caveney was willing, if they could find someone to replace him. "How about my kid brother?" Vince suggested.

Ike thought it over. Finally he shrugged. "It's too late in the season to hurt us. Get the kid a uniform."

Joe could hardly believe his good fortune. Here he was, actually playing with the Seals!

His first time at bat he hit a triple. Later he got another hit. It was a good showing.

In the field, Joe didn't do so well. He knew he had a powerful throwing arm, and he was afraid of losing control. The first time the ball came his way, he tossed it lightly to the first baseman. It barely got there. "Hey, kid, you throw like a girl!" the other players jeered.

"Well," Joe said to himself, "maybe I'm not as strong as I think."

The next time he got the ball, he threw it with the full force of his arm. It went sizzling past the first baseman into the stand for an error.

The next spring, Joe was invited to the Seals' training school. His throwing arm was still wild, but he had the bat under control. And when the 1933 season opened, the Seals offered him a regular contract. Now there were two DiMaggios in professional baseball.

For the first few days, Joe sat on the bench, awaiting his chance. Then it came. "Get in there and pinch hit," Ike Caveney ordered.

Joe took a turn at bat. And when the inning was over, the manager said, "Go on out and play in the outfield."

Joe stared in astonishment. "But I've never been an outfielder!" he protested.

"Believe me, Joe," said Ike, "with that

Young Joe DiMaggio, record hitter for the San Francisco Seals, at the age of nineteen

throwing arm, the outfield is where you belong."

So Joe trotted out to the outfield, and there he stayed. Ike Caveney was right. Joe's mighty arm was exactly suited to the outfield. As he matured, he gained control. Soon he was scooping up line drives and sending the ball whistling back into the infield. He caught many an unwary base runner with his lightning returns.

But batting was still Joe's specialty. He had developed a wide stance and tough, swift wrist action. When he connected, the ball really traveled. More than that, you could count on Joe for a hit.

"Have you heard about that kid DiMaggio?" San Francisco fans began to ask one another. "He hasn't missed getting a hit in twenty straight games."

"Oh, he's just a rookie, batting over his head," some people scoffed.

But Joe's bat showed the skeptics that they were wrong. Game after game he came to the plate, set himself with feet apart, cocked his bat, and waited for the pitch. Then, *crack!* another ball went slamming against the outfield wall. Soon his hitting streak reached thirty games.

Now the whole Pacific Coast League was excited. Fans crowded into ball parks to see how long Joe could keep going. "That makes thirty-one games!"

When the streak got to forty games, sportswriters started talking about the record. In 1914, the year Joe was born, Jack Ness had hit safely in forty-nine games. It was a record for the Pacific Coast League.

"Do you think Joe can beat the league record?" fans asked one another.

Joe worked the streak up to forty-eight games. Then came the game that could tie Jack Ness's record. Joe could not seem to get a hit. In the ninth inning, six men were ahead of him in the batting order. It looked as if the streak were broken.

One teammate slapped young Joe on the shoulder. "The team is behind you, kid. You'll get your chance if we have to break our necks."

Sure enough, all six men managed to get on base. When Joe came to bat, he hit a double.

In the following game, he got another hit, breaking the old record. Then young Joe went blazing on until he had hit safely in sixty-one games. By then fans all over the country had their eyes on the San Francisco boy. Major-league scouts came running. Even Papa DiMaggio was impressed. "Maybe this baseball isn't so bad," he admitted cautiously.

For Joe there was only one sad thing about 1933. The Seals decided they didn't

Seal bosses with DiMaggio, from left: "Doc" Strub, Joe, Charles Graham, and Caveney

need Vince. Joe's big brother went to another Pacific Coast team.

Things looked good for Joe as the 1934 season got started. Big-league teams were looking him over. Even the Yankees were interested. "I'd sure like to play for the Yankees," he confided wistfully to young Dom.

Then in June Joe twisted his knee. He thought nothing of it at first. But soon it hurt so much that he could not play. At season's end, he was still sitting on the Seals' bench.

Baseball scouts shook their heads. Nobody wanted a player with a bad knee. "DiMaggio's just a one-season flash," some reported to their clubs. "Forget him."

Joe tried not to lose hope. But it was hard waiting when everyone was turning away from him.

Then one night came the telephone call from the Seals' president to tell Joe that the Yankees still had faith in him. They had so much faith that they expected him to replace the great Babe Ruth!

First, Joe needed a further year of seasoning with the Seals. Then, in February, 1936, Joe DiMaggio went east to report to the Yankees.

The pressure was on, right from the start of spring training. "So you're the big hitter from the Coast," said reporters. "Do you really think you can take over from the Babe?"

For all the fame that surrounded him, Joe was still shy and tongue-tied. "I can try," he muttered.

Questions came at him from all sides: "Can you hit major-league pitching?"

"Yankee Stadium is a big ball park. Do you think you can cover your share of that outfield?"

"Will you be bothered by those tough New York fans?"

Stories cropped up in the newspapers. "DiMaggio is the greatest rookie since Ty Cobb," some sportswriters proclaimed. Others predicted that Joe would never take Ruth's place. Still others compared him with Lou Gehrig, Tris Speaker, Joe Jackson, and other greats. "DiMaggio," wrote one reporter, "is the Yankees' only hope for the pennant."

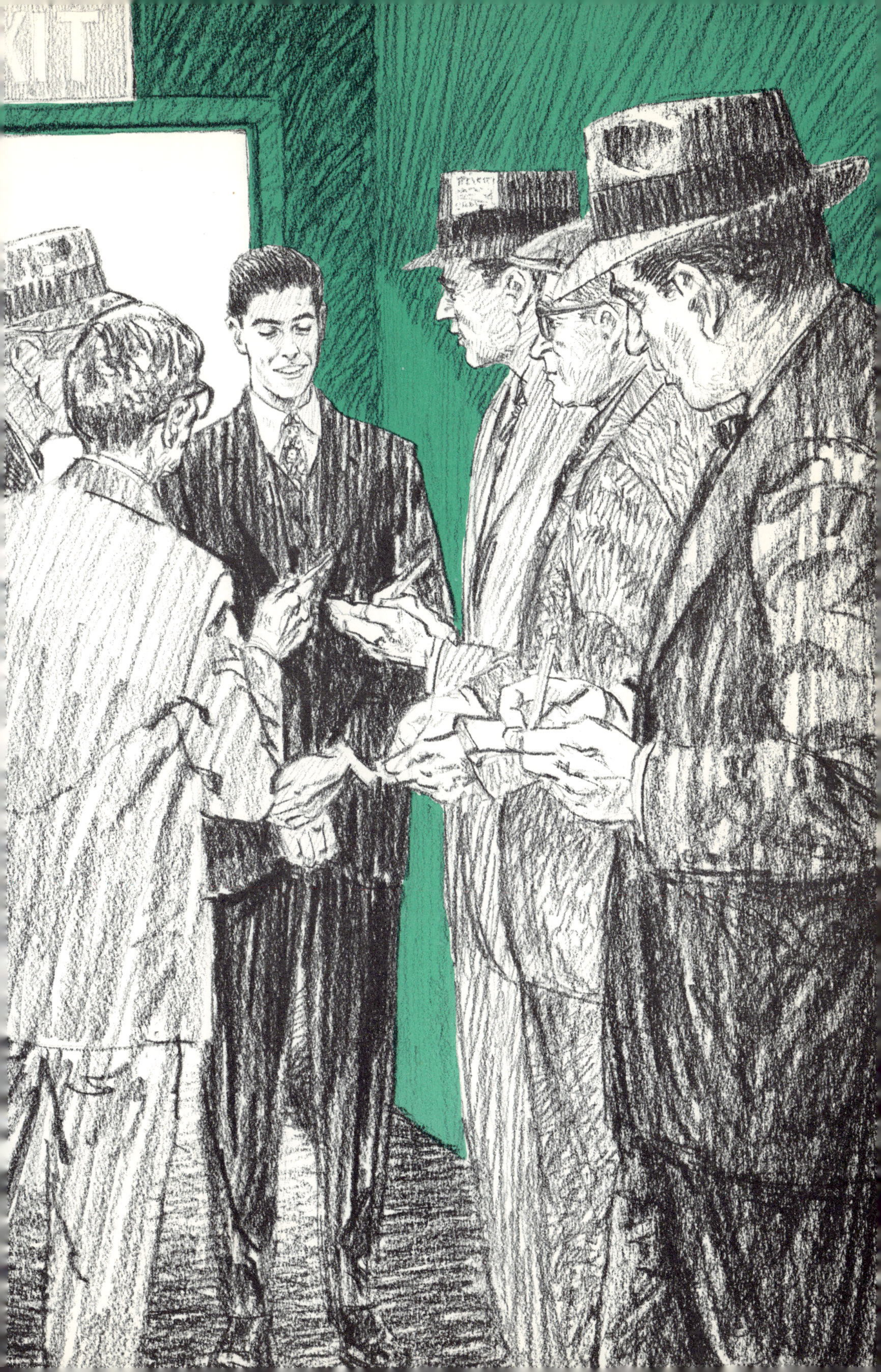

It was frightening, the things they expected of him. It was flattering, too. But Joe kept his head. "I'm here to do my best," he said simply.

Yes, DiMaggio could hit major-league pitching. He got two singles and a triple in his first game.

Yes, the San Francisco boy could field big Yankee Stadium. In his second game, Joe threw from left field all the way to home plate and pegged the runner out.

No, Joe wasn't bothered by tough New York fans. In fact, they loved the modest young player. He soon had his own cheering section.

He played so well that in July he was named to the All-Star team. No other rookie had ever been so honored.

All through the summer, the pace kept up. Fans watched Joe. Sportswriters gathered when he appeared.

Babe Ruth had loved excitement and attention. But Joe didn't know how to answer fans and reporters. "Why can't they let me alone?" he often wondered. Like it or not, everything he did was publicized.

The Yankees had not won a pennant in three years. Now, with Joe on the team, they not only won but ended up with a nineteen-game lead. Then they went on to win the World Series.

"Young DiMaggio has given the Yankees new spirit," one writer declared. "Without him, they could never have won."

Joe's hometown agreed. When "the second Babe Ruth" returned to San Francisco, he was met by a brass band. Nobody was prouder of Joe than Papa DiMaggio. "Baseball, that's my sport," he said, hugging Joe.

The pressure eased up a little the next year. But Joe was still the center of attention. Fans were still comparing him to Ruth.

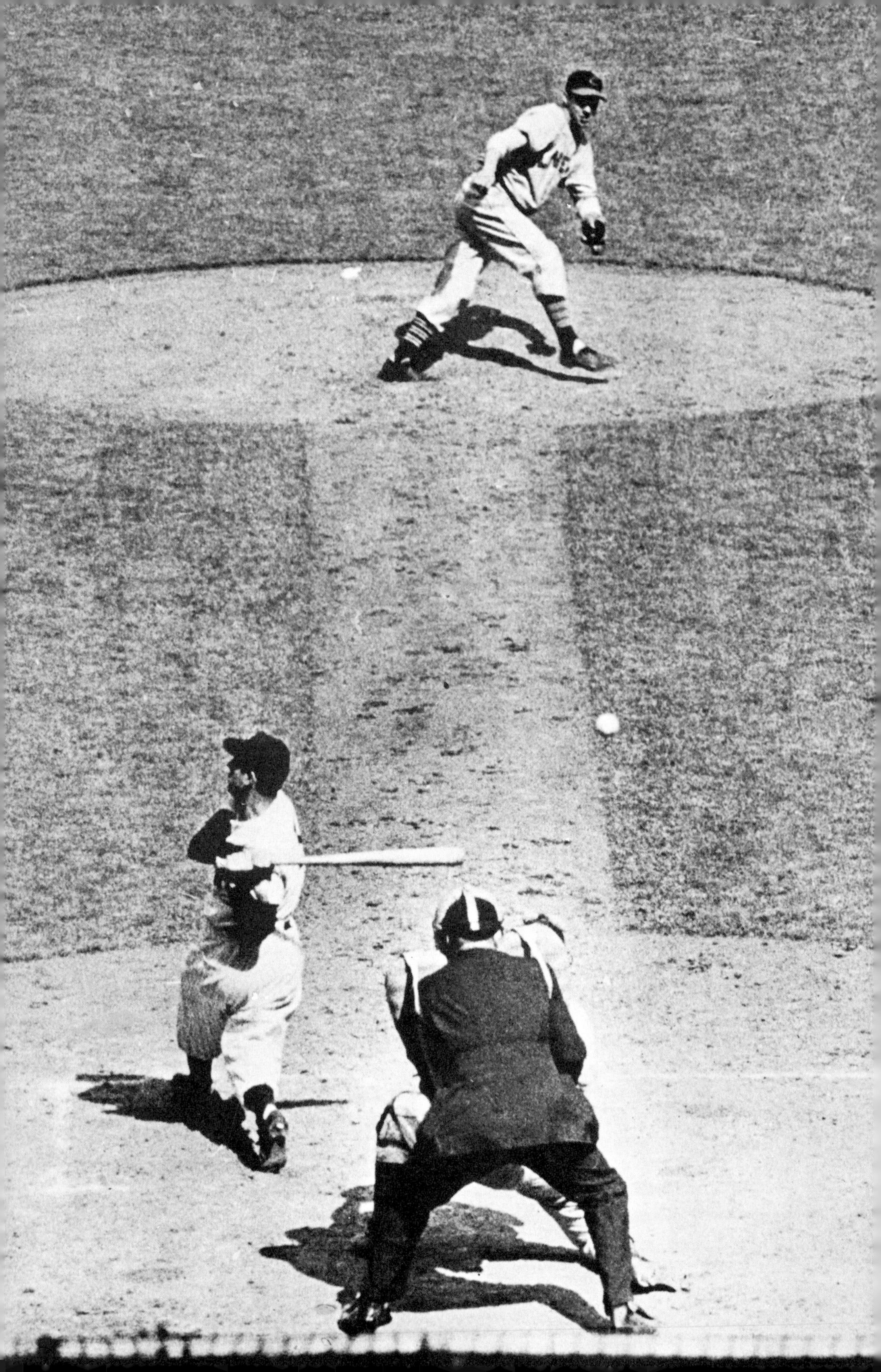

Yankee Stadium's short right-field wall favored left-handed hitters like the Babe. Joe batted right-handed. Nevertheless he racked up an average of .346 in 1937. And in the seasons that followed, he continued to hit in the three hundreds and twice led his league in batting.

Many experts believed his fielding was even better than his hitting. "He makes impossible catches," said one writer. "But often no one notices it, because he makes fielding look so easy."

"Joe is one of the finest base runners in the game," said another. "He's always trying for that extra base."

Meanwhile, Vince and then Dominic DiMaggio moved up to the major leagues. Vince played for National League teams, but Dom was bought by the Boston Red Sox, one of the Yankees' most powerful opponents.

Yankee star DiMaggio, left, connects with a ball pitched by Bob Feller.

Then in 1941, history began to repeat itself for Joe.

On May 15, in a game with the Chicago White Sox, Joe got a hit. By itself that was nothing special. But he hit safely in the following game, too, and in the one after that. Before long another hitting streak was on.

Joe didn't like to talk about it. Neither did his teammates. But everyone else did. "Well, Joe DiMaggio has made it twenty straight," people said on the street and in the subways.

"Today's hit makes it twenty-five in a row for Joe," newspapers reported.

"Here's a bulletin from Yankee Stadium," radio announcers said. "Joe DiMaggio has just hit safely in game number thirty."

Soon people began to talk about DiMaggio setting a major-league record. In 1898, Wee Willie Keeler hit safely in forty-four games, the all-time high for the majors. Could Joe do better?

Game followed game, each adding one to his total. Excitement mounted. Yankee fans flocked to the ball park or stuck close to their radios.

Manager Joe McCarthy wanted his star to have every chance. Usually managers give batters instructions on how to hit and what kind of balls to watch out for. But McCarthy decided to let Joe use his own judgment.

On June 21, Joe hit safely in the thirty-fourth game, topping the National League record. Eight days later, he broke George Sisler's American League record of forty-one games. All that remained was Keeler's, set in the days when there was only one major league. On July 1, the Yankees were scheduled to play a doubleheader with the Boston Red Sox.

Joe got two hits in the first game, running his streak to forty-three. The second game was called at the end of five innings because of rain. But not before Joe had gotten his hit, for forty-four.

"He's done it!" cried delighted fans. "He's tied Keeler's record!"

"Yes, but can he break it?"

"Tomorrow will tell."

July 2 dawned bright and hot. Joe tried

not to be nervous. He called Dom at the Red Sox' hotel and invited him to have dinner after the game. "All right," Dom joked, "but don't expect any favors from me on the field."

In the first inning, Joe hit a long fly to right field, which was taken for the out. His second time at bat he caught a beautiful pitch. Back and back it went, toward center field. Joe was sure he had a double

Joe, above, chooses just the right bat. Below, he hits safely in his 44th consecutive game.

—at least. Then at the last minute, the Red Sox fielder made a spectacular catch.

"That was your own brother who caught that!" cried pitcher Lefty Gomez as Joe returned to the bench.

"Yes," he agreed with a rueful grin. "At least it shows that baseball is an honest game."

In the fifth inning, Joe came to bat once more. The crowd was tense and quiet in the 94-degree heat. Veteran sportswriters held their breath. Nine thousand pairs of eyes were on the tall figure at the plate. Joe took his wide stance and waited, bat poised.

Heber Newsome pitched one bad ball, then a second. "Are they going to walk me?" Joe wondered.

But, no, the third pitch was good. Joe fouled it off, and the crowd groaned. Then came the fourth pitch.

Joe swung from his heels. There was a *crack*! The ball went up and out, far over Dom DiMaggio's head. It landed in the left-field stands for a home run.

Keeler's record, which had stood for forty-three years, was broken. And by a home run!

The grinning Joe was mobbed as he

crossed the plate. "You did it! You did it!" teammates cried.

Lefty Gomez threw an arm around him. "*That's* how to keep Dom's hands off the ball!"

Reporters and radio announcers sent the news out across the nation. "A lot of people have called Joe 'a second Babe Ruth,'"

one sportswriter wrote. "But after today, Joe will stand alone."

Joe had a nickname of his own now: the Yankee Clipper.

Joe went on to run his hitting streak to fifty-six games. He went on to play thirteen seasons of major-league ball. He went on to win three Most Valuable Player awards and two batting championships. He went on to spark the Yankees to ten pennants. And no one expected him to be anything but Joe DiMaggio, the Yankee Clipper.

Often the highest praise showered on Joe DiMaggio has been for his workmanship. He did not make scenes or cause trouble or demand the spotlight. In his quiet way, Joe was all ballplayer, and nobody admired him more than his own teammates.

Joe's last seasons were shortened by injuries and illness. He often kept playing in spite of pain. "If Joe can walk, Joe will play," a friend once said. But at last he was forced to end his playing days.

He put away his Yankee uniform. He returned to San Francisco and went into business. But he never stopped being a baseball hero. Like Babe Ruth's, his name is known to many who have never seen him play.

A few years after Joe left baseball, a reporter was questioning Yankee manager Casey Stengel. "Casey, who's the greatest Yankee of them all?"

Stengel had spent fifty years in baseball. He had seen Gehrig and Ruth. He had managed Mantle and Berra. But after a moment of thought, he answered, "I would have to say DiMaggio. Joe was great doing everything."

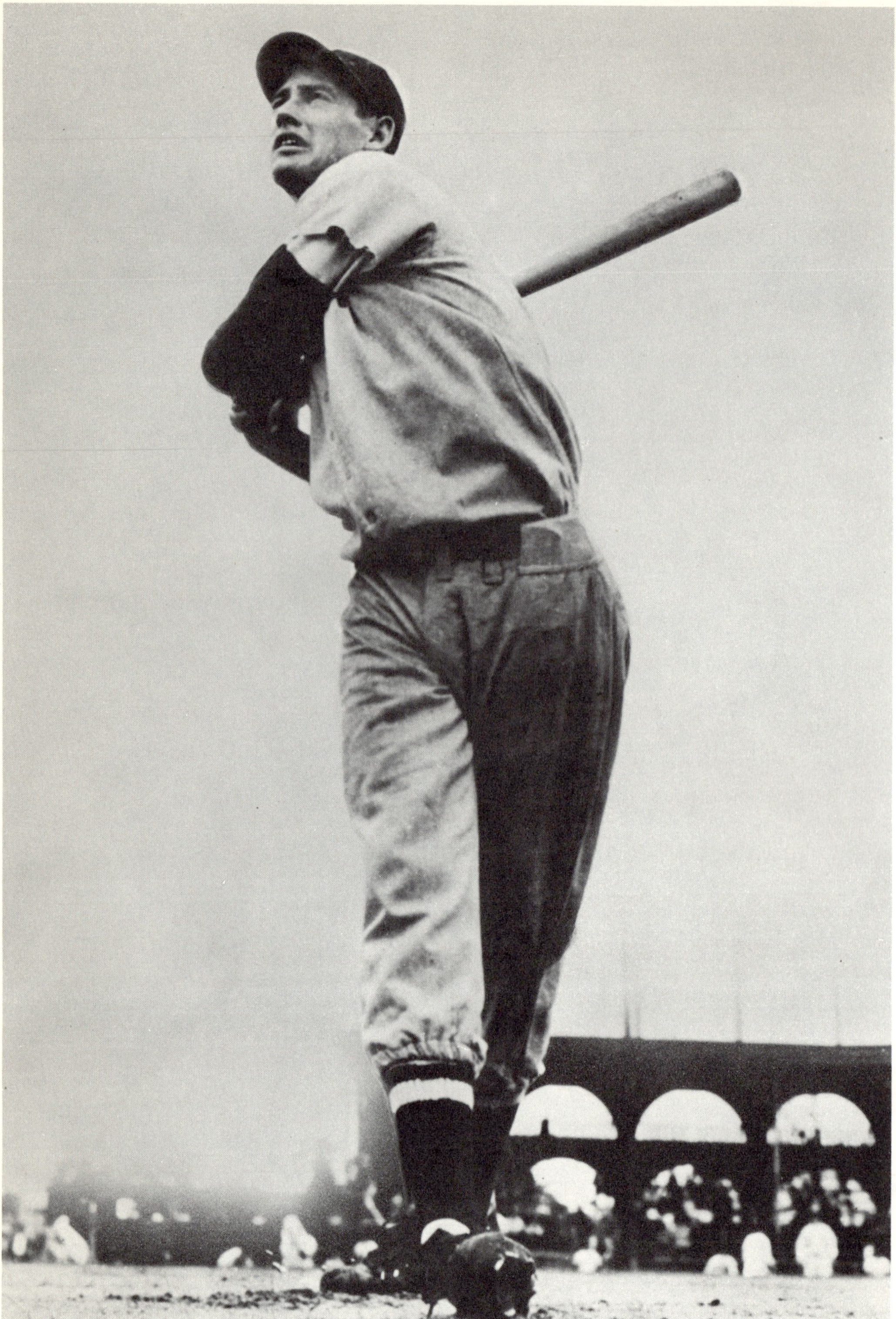

All He's Got: Ted Williams

The Red Sox manager took his young outfielder by the arm. "Sit out these last two games, Ted," he urged. "Don't risk your record."

The young outfielder shook his head. "I wouldn't quit now for anything."

It was the last day of the 1941 baseball season. The Athletics were playing a doubleheader against the Boston Red Sox at Shibe Park, Philadelphia. But few people cared about the game itself.

"I came here to see baseball history made," one fan said flatly.

His friend nodded. "I'm a Philadelphia rooter," he said. "But I sure hope the Boston kid makes it."

The Boston kid was Theodore Samuel Williams. He was trying to finish the 1941 baseball season with a .400 batting average.

Since 1887, only eleven major-league players had earned averages higher than .400. Ted's average had been over .400 all season. But in the last few weeks it had slowly slipped down to .399½. Perhaps this season Ted would fail.

"They don't count halves," said one reporter in the press box. "That will go into the books as four hundred even. With only two more games left, the kid ought to stay out and play it safe."

A Boston reporter smiled. "Ted never plays things safe. He always gives all he's got."

The first game began with Dick Fowler pitching. Ted came to bat. The first two pitches were balls. Then came the third pitch. Ted swung, and the ball whizzed past the infielders for a single.

Reporters did some quick arithmetic. "That brings him up to four hundred even," one said. "Let's see if he can keep it up."

Ted came to bat again in the fourth inning. That time the ball went over the right center-field wall for a home run.

"That makes it four-oh-two," said the reporters. "Come on, Ted baby. Keep going."

For his third trip to the plate, Ted faced a new pitcher, Porter Vaughan. He hit a single.

"That's four-oh-three!"

Ted came to bat for the fourth time. The ball traveled over the first baseman's head for another single.

"That makes it four-oh-four!"

In his fifth time at bat, Ted got on base through a fielder's error. It did not count.

"Well," said the reporters as the first game ended, "Ted is all set now. He can go without a hit in the next game and still be over four hundred."

But the Boston man shook his head. "I tell you, this kid is stubborn as a mule. He's never going to stop trying for those base hits."

And so it proved. In the second and last game, Ted came to bat three times. Once he popped out. Once he singled. Once he doubled. Then the game ended.

"Well, that does it!" someone cried. "The kid has hit four-oh-six for the season!"

Some reporters grabbed telephones, while others rushed to their typewriters. Fans poured out of the stands and onto the field. Players, umpires, and officials crowded around Ted.

"Kid," someone cried into the boy's ear, "you're the greatest hitter in baseball!"

Ted grinned from ear to ear. He had wanted to hear those words as far back as he could remember.

Ted had started practicing to be a ballplayer as soon as he was old enough to hold a bat. When he had no baseball, he swung at tennis balls or balls made of rags. He raced to school early so he could play ball before classes started.

Little by little, Ted developed a loose and powerful swing. "Who taught you to swing like that?" a playground instructor asked him once.

"I taught myself."

"Well, keep it up."

Ted played on his school teams in junior and senior high school. He also played on an American Legion team and on a team sponsored by a grocery. During his last two years in high school, he batted .583 and .406. Big-league scouts watched him play and showed interest in signing him up.

At seventeen, Ted Williams was signed to play with the San Diego Padres, a minor-league team. He was a tall, skinny boy. To some he looked too frail to play ball. But others saw greatness in him.

A rival manager watched him bat one

day. The manager, Lefty O'Doul, knew something about batting. In his playing days he had twice been batting champion of the National League.

"Don't let them change that swing, kid," Lefty told young Ted. "Stay as sweet as you are."

Ted laughed and promised not to change.

Young Williams had two years with San Diego. Then the Boston Red Sox bought him. They liked his hitting style, but his fielding was awkward.

"You need a little more seasoning, Ted," said Joe Cronin, the Red Sox manager. "We're sending you back to the minor leagues."

Ted's new team was the Minneapolis Millers. When the season opened Ted went game after game without a hit. He had a quick temper, and his failures made him storm furiously.

"Take it easy, kid," his teammates advised.

But Ted paid no attention. In his anger, he tore up towels and deliberately broke bats. Finally one day he drove his fist at a big glass water jug. The jug smashed. Broken glass cut him across the wrist.

"You're in luck, Ted," the manager said grimly as the gash was bandaged. "You might have been hurt badly."

Ted was ashamed of his tantrum. "I want to make good," he explained. "I want to be the greatest batter in the world."

"Okay, but from now on, do your smashing out there on the field."

The slump soon ended, and Ted's batting became the terror of the minor leagues. But he was still weak in fielding.

His long arms and legs were hard to manage. He couldn't stop and turn easily. Besides, he often forgot all about watching for flies and practiced batting instead.

Once a high fly headed Ted's way. There he stood in left field, glove off, swinging an imaginary bat. "Hey, Ted, wake up!" yelled his teammates.

He came to just in time to make the catch.

But Ted's batting more than made up for his fielding. At the end of the season, he was leading his league, and the Red Sox recalled him.

Ted hit .327 in 1939, his first year with the Red Sox. Babe Ruth said he was the rookie of the year. The second year his average went up to .344.

It took work to keep hitting at that rate. Ted did exercises to build up his arm muscles. He asked advice from Jimmy Foxx, Bill Dickey, Hank Greenberg, and other famous hitters. He was out of bed at seven every morning, practicing his swing.

He made a careful study of pitchers, noting each one's special tricks. He knew by heart almost every pitch thrown at him.

"You can only get Williams out when you're new to him," a rival pitcher explained to a reporter. "Once he knows you, you can't fool him anymore."

Ted worked at his fielding, too, but he remained awkward for a long time. Many

Williams, right, played for the Padres in 1937. Two years later, below, he was a Boston rookie.

fans thought he wasn't trying. If he missed a ground ball, they booed him. If a fly got lost in the sun, they called him names.

Most players pay no attention to razzing. But Ted was sensitive. "I always let them know I'm out there," he said. His quick temper led him into several arguments with Boston fans.

Once he foolishly decided to get back at some rude fans. "I'll strike out deliberately," he told himself.

But Ted could not do things halfway even when he wanted to. He tried to foul off the next pitch. Instead, he hit a double.

Reporters liked to tease Ted. Once they followed him on a visit to his uncle, who was a fireman. Ted found the older man sitting contentedly in the sun before the firehouse. "I wish I could take it easy like that," he joked. "Maybe I'll quit baseball and be a fireman."

Reporters wrote seriously, "Ted Williams threatens to quit playing baseball and become a fireman."

Rival teams leaped at the chance to taunt Williams. They blew whistles when he appeared. They yelled, "Fire!" Jimmy Dykes, manager of the Chicago White Sox, handed out firemen's helmets to his players. When Ted came to bat, the White Sox put on the helmets, clanged bells, and imitated sirens.

Ted didn't mind jokes from fellow players. He laughed and went on hitting. Soon rival pitchers became the real victims. "Try pulling a fire alarm!" the Red Sox jeered at them. "Maybe Ted will hop aboard the truck!"

By 1941, there were more cheers than jeers. Ted ended the season with his record batting average of .406. And more than one expert was saying, "Williams is the greatest hitter in baseball!"

Ted Williams took time out from baseball during World War II to serve as a pilot.

The Japanese attack on Pearl Harbor followed close on the heels of Ted's big triumph. Near the end of the 1942 season he enlisted in the Navy as an aviation cadet. In May, 1944, he received his wings as a lieutenant in the U. S. Marine Corps. He served as a flight instructor until the end of the war.

Ted's first postwar season was 1946, one of his best. His big day was the All-Star game. He hit one homer early in the game. Then he came to bat again in the eighth inning.

Rip Sewall of the Pirates was pitching for the National League. "Rip has this special pitch. He calls it the 'ephus' ball," Ted was told. "It arches high and comes in slowly. Even when you hit it, it hardly travels out of the infield."

Ted was curious. "I'd like to try one," he answered.

Sewall was willing. His first "ephus" was a called strike. Then he pitched another. Ted took a forward hop, swung, and sent the famed "ephus" ball right out of the ball park.

Rival managers tried many ways of stopping Ted's big bat. Lou Boudreau of Cleveland had the best scheme. Most of Ted's

This well-known batting style made Wiliams the despair of any opposing team's pitchers.

hits were to right field or right center field. Boudreau pulled his fielders over toward the right. There were no bare spots where Ted could poke a hit, unless he batted toward left field.

"You can hit to left," advisers urged. "Maybe you won't hit the ball so far, but a single is better than nothing."

Stubborn and hot-tempered as usual, Ted answered, "I'm not paid to hit singles."

The Red Sox led the league in 1946. In September they played a game with Cleveland that would clinch the pennant. It was 0–0 in the ninth inning. Then Ted came to bat.

The Cleveland fielders moved over into "the Williams shift." Red Embree pitched. And Ted did what he said he wouldn't do: he hit to left.

"Hey! Look at that ball travel!" screamed Boston fans.

Long-legged Ted slides into home plate in time to score a Red Sox run.

While the Cleveland fielders scrambled for the ball, Ted raced around the bases on his long legs. He had to slide for home, but he made it. It was baseball's most difficult hit, an inside-the-park home run.

That home run won the game, and that game clinched the pennant.

The World Series in 1946 was the only one Ted ever played in. He hit poorly. But he pulled out of the slump in 1947 and won his third batting championship.

Batting still came first with Ted. He practiced constantly and worked hard to keep himself in trim. When he took batting practice, other players stopped what they were doing to watch. They only did that for a master batsman.

Ted's fielding had improved over the years. He seldom missed balls anymore. But some people refused to admit the improvement. "Williams has no team spirit," they complained. "He loafs. He doesn't care whether he catches balls or not."

Ted refused to defend himself against such charges. But his boss backed him up. "He has a big glove out there," said Joe Cronin, meaning that Ted covered a lot of outfield territory. But fans weren't satisfied.

Then in the 1950 All-Star game, Ralph Kiner hit a long fly to left. Ted had to run fast and make a great leap to get his glove on the ball. And as he caught it, his elbow cracked against the wall.

"Did you hurt yourself, Ted?" a teammate asked as they changed sides.

"It's all right. I can finish the game."

Ted stuck it out for eight innings. He made another running catch. He got one hit and popped out twice. But finally he asked to be relieved. They then discovered that he had broken his elbow in that first-inning catch.

"Now nobody can call Ted a lazy fielder," one reporter said of the incident. "But it's a tough way to have to prove yourself."

Four years later Ted proved again that he had hustle. He was chasing a fly ball in spring practice. He tried too hard, fell, and broke his collarbone.

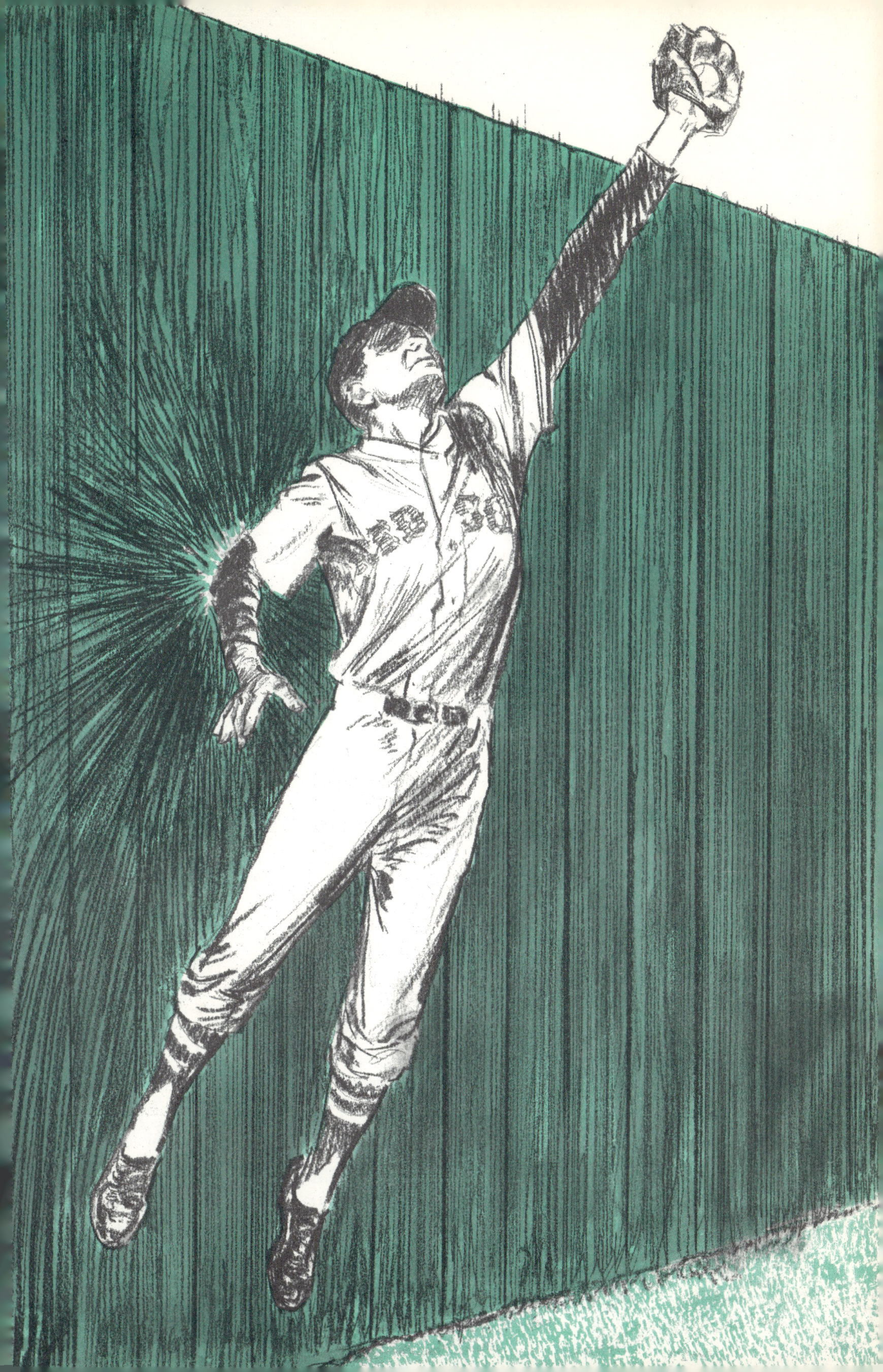

Ted didn't like people to pry into his private life. He even tried to keep his good deeds secret. When he went to visit sick children, he always sneaked off quietly.

"That's my business," he replied gruffly when reporters questioned him.

His favorite charity was the Jimmy Fund for children's cancer research. His help brought the fund nearly half a million dollars in contributions.

In 1952, the Marine Corps called Ted back into active service. He was sent to Korea as a jet bomber pilot. He flew thirty-nine missions against the enemy.

One day Captain Williams' plane was badly shot up in action. His radio and other instruments went dead. His brakes wouldn't work, and he couldn't lower the landing gear. His commanding officer signaled him to jump, but he thought he could make it home safely.

As he flew over the landing field, other planes scattered. He brought the plane in on its belly. It skidded and swerved. When at last it lurched to a stop, Ted was surrounded by smoke and flames.

"My gosh, it's on fire!" he cried. He leaped out and ran before the flames could reach the fuel. "If I'd known it was on fire," he said later, "I'd have listened to my commanding officer."

Ted was thirty-five years old when he returned to baseball. Most players are retired by then, but Ted still had a lot of baseball in him. He won two more batting championships, beating out young Mickey Mantle. He might have been champion two other years, too, but to qualify for the award, a player must have been at bat four hundred times. Nervous pitchers had given him too many walks, which did not count as times at bat.

Ted Williams gives some professional tips to a few admiring fans.

"Think of that!" marveled a rival pitcher. "Williams is forty years old, and the pitchers are still scared to pitch to him!"

But finally Ted decided that 1960 would have to be his last season.

Ted Williams had made a great record. His lifetime batting average was .344, two points higher than the great Babe Ruth. He belonged to that small group of men who have hit over .400. He won six American League batting championships. Four times he led the league in home runs. Twice he won baseball's Triple Crown, ranking first in batting average, home runs, and runs batted in. Five times he was voted the league's Most Valuable Player. And, proving that he had intelligence as well as skill, in 1969 he was brought out of retirement to manage the Washington Senators.

"Williams lost five years to the Marine

Corps," experts point out. "He suffered a lot of bad injuries. Pitchers gave him all those walks. Think what records he might have set if he'd had better breaks!"

Ted came to bat for the last time in Fenway Park, Boston. It was exactly nineteen years to the day since that doubleheader in Shibe Park. And he was still giving all he had.

His first time at bat, pitcher Jack Fisher of Baltimore walked him. He popped out the second and third times he was up. Then in the eighth inning, Ted Williams came to bat for the last time in his playing career.

Fisher wound up and threw. Ted swung—the same loose, beautiful swing he had developed on the San Diego playgrounds. And the ball went out of the park.